# Toffee's Great Rescue

The Courage of a Pup and the Power of Community

Author
Richard Breitbach
Illustrator
Nancy Finnegan

WALDENHOUSE PUBLISHERS
WALDEN TENNESSEE

**Toffee's Great Rescue:** The Courage of a Pup and the Power of Community

Copyright ©2025 Richard Allen Breitbach, 1959

All rights reserved. No part of this book may be reproduced in any form or by any electronic or mechanical means including information storage and retrieval systems, without permission in writing from the publisher. The only exception is by a reviewer, who may quote short excerpts in a review.

This is a work of creative nonfiction. Some parts have been fictionalized in varying degrees for various purposes.

Illustrations by Nancy Finnegan

Comic Sans on 70# LSI archival white

Published by Waldenhouse Publishers, Inc.

100 Clegg Street, Signal Mountain, Tennessee 37377 USA

www.waldenhouse.com    423-886-2721

Printed in the United States of America

ISBN 978-1-947589-87-2 hardcover

ISBN 978-1-947589-88-9 softcover

Library of Congress Control Number 2025939571

*Toffee's Great Rescue* is an uplifting tale of a blind and deaf puppy who, after falling into a hidden crevice, inspires a community to unite in her rescue. Through courage, teamwork and determination, Toffee's story showcases the power of hope and the strength of working together to overcome challenges. -- Provided by publisher

JNF003060    JUVENILE NONFICTION / Animals / Dogs

JNF053180    JUVENILE NONFICTION / Disability

JNF081000    JUVENILE NONFICTION / Community & Neighbors

# Dedication

This book is dedicated to the volunteers
whose relentless efforts
gave a tiny blind and deaf puppy
a second chance at life.

# Acknowledgments

Special recognition goes to the incredible team at Roto-Rooter of Huntsville, Alabama, whose staunch commitment and expertise made Toffee's rescue possible. Their remarkable efforts serve as a testament to the strength of community and the power of teamwork. Thank you for being true heroes.

**T**his is the heartwarming story of Toffee, a remarkable puppy whose unwavering courage and bravery brought a community together in the face of a great challenge.

It all began on a peaceful farm in North Alabama. In the quiet embrace of an old barn, where beams of sunlight filtered through wooden slats and specks of dust danced in golden rays, a litter of tiny puppies nestled up on the dirt floor next to an old tractor.

The farmer, a man with strong, gentle hands and a compassionate heart, discovered the puppies by chance.

Concern etched across his face; he made a weary call to the local veterinarian. "I can't give them what they need," he admitted. "They deserve a real chance."

Moved by urgency, the veterinarian sprang into action.

After a series of calls, relief washed over her when *A New Leash on Life* in Huntsville, AL, responded enthusiastically. "We'll take them," they assured.

The puppies were soon given names inspired by delicious flavors of ice cream: Toffee, Chocolate Chip, Cotton Candy, Snickerdoodle, Brickle, Vanilla, Oreo, and Espresso.

Each name reflected their unique personalities, adding to the joy they brought to the pet rescue center. The puppies required extra attention and tender care, particularly little Toffee, who was deaf and barely able to see.

Caring for the puppies was a challenge with the rescue center at full capacity. Karen, a dedicated volunteer known for her tireless devotion, never hesitated. "I'll bring them home," she declared.

She transformed her house into a sanctuary with soft blankets and lullabies.

Despite her inability to hear and her impaired vision, Toffee's spirit remained unbroken.

Guided by her nose and the vibrations of her siblings' playful steps, she joined every game, her tiny tail wagging wildly with joy.

Each evening, the puppies explored the backyard, their playground of adventures. One warm June night, under a canopy of stars, Toffee ventured out with her usual enthusiasm.

The grass tickled her paws, and the summer breeze carried scents of the world beyond her reach.

Then, in the blink of an eye, Toffee was gone.

Toffee had stumbled into a deep crevice hidden among the rocks. She tumbled downward, her tiny heart pounding as she landed on a cold, uneven rock shelf. For a moment, the world spun around her.

It wasn't fear that gripped her, but curiosity. Toffee explored her new surroundings.

Where were her brothers and sisters? She shivered, feeling all alone. Her tummy rumbled as she curled up on the rock ledge, tired and hungry, unaware of the panic above.

Karen's heart dropped when she saw Toffee disappear. "Toffee!" she called into the night, her voice shaking. Silence answered. Desperation rising, she called the fire department. Within minutes, a team arrived, their faces set with determination. *"We'll find Toffee,"* one assured her.

But this rescue was unlike any other. Traditional search methods wouldn't work — Toffee couldn't hear their calls or see their lights, and time was slipping away.

The next morning, as the first rays of sunshine touched the town, the community rallied to help Toffee. Word spread quickly, and neighbors, friends, and even strangers soon joined the effort.

They worked side by side, their hearts shining as brightly as the morning light, determined to bring Toffee back to safety.

By noon, the breakthrough came. A plumber, drawn by the urgency of the rescue mission, had an idea.

"Let's use a small camera," he suggested. "Designed to work in tight spaces—we might be able to locate her."

With precise care, the team lowered the camera into the crevice. A live feed flickered across the computer screen as rocky walls and shadows moved past.

At forty-eight feet, a small pale figure came into view —Toffee, curled up and fast asleep.

Above, cheers erupted. "We found her!"

But the hardest part was still ahead.

Reaching her at forty-eight feet underground was a daunting task. The narrow crevice was lined with jagged edges, determined to hinder every rescue attempt.

The team devised a plan: they crafted a strong, soft net attached to flexible pipes, perfect for gently lifting her to safety. They added biscuits, hoping to lure her in.

Finally, they lowered the net near Toffee. The rescuers watched the screen as they saw her sniff the biscuits. Toffee hesitated. Then, the net brushed softly against her fur. Sensing something was wrong, she quickly backed away to her rocky ledge.

Hunger gnawed at her, but fear held her back. She had learned to be cautious.

They needed a better plan.

Hours passed. Frustration mounted. Then, a small voice cut through the tension.

"Maybe she doesn't like the food you're using," suggested Lily, a young girl clutching a stuffed animal.

Her innocent wisdom sparked an idea. What if they used something irresistible? Steve, a seasoned rescuer, snapped his fingers.

"Sardines! I have a can in my truck."

The team gathered around as he opened the can, and a strong scent spread through the cool night air. "This is a dog's dream," Steve stated with a grin. "No pup can resist that smell."

Moments later, the net was lowered again, carrying the tempting bait. Volunteers, neighbors, and news crews stood side by side, eyes fixed on the monitor as the net settled softly near Toffee.

Toffee lifted her head, her nose twitching. What was that smell? It was wonderful, unlike anything she'd ever smelled before. The hunger was too strong now.

Gathering all her courage, with cautious steps, she moved toward the net. At last, Toffee reached the source — a delicious treat that promised to satisfy her hunger. Then, in a swift motion, the net closed gently around her.

Panic flared as she struggled, but there was nothing she could do to free herself.

"We got her!" Steve announced, his voice breaking with emotion. A wave of relief swept over the crowd, but the job wasn't done yet.

Carefully, Toffee's slow ascent began. Every foot gained was met with held breath.

"Forty feet... thirty... twenty... ten..."

Finally, at five feet, Steve reached down, his arms stretching into the darkness. His fingers closed around the net. With one smooth motion, he lifted Toffee into the open air.

For a moment, there was stunned silence.

Then, an eruption of cheers. Toffee was finally rescued.

Karen rushed forward, tears spilling as she took Toffee into her arms.

"Oh, sweet girl, you're safe," she whispered, pressing Toffee close

Lily, the little girl whose idea had made all the difference, beamed as she gently stroked Toffee's fur.

"She's a brave one," she said proudly.

Toffee's story spread like wildfire. Social media buzzed with *BringToffeeHome*. The rescuers' faces glowed with happiness as they celebrated their hard work. Together, they had turned an impossible situation into a triumph of joy and happiness.

Television stations broadcast the rescue, and the story of the little blind and deaf puppy who had united a community in hope and determination touched hearts far and wide.

That night, Toffee curled up between her foster parents, safe at last.

As sleep embraced her, her tiny body relaxed into the warmth of love and security.

The power of community had given her a second chance, proving that no challenge is too big with teamwork and purpose.

Toffee's bravery and will to survive inspired everyone and reminded them of the courage that lives within even the smallest of hearts.

# Afterword

Toffee's rescue story is based on events after the tiny pup fell into a crevice in late June 2018. The rescue mission for Toffee became a powerful display of unity as the Huntsville, Alabama, community came together to save the blind and deaf puppy. The fire department, police department, and local rescue experts coordinated their efforts, facing the challenge of locating Toffee. After nearly three days, the rescuers finally brought her back to the surface. You can learn more about the rescue at **www.toffeetherescuedpup.com**

Heroes from Huntsville Fire Department

Can you read Toffee's bandana?

www.ingramcontent.com/pod-product-compliance
Lightning Source LLC
Chambersburg PA
CBHW040002290426
43673CB00077B/320